Tablescapes

SETTING THE TABLE WITH STYLE

KIMBERLY SCHLEGEL WHITMAN

GIBBS SMITH
TO ENRICH AND INSPIRE HUMANKIND
Salt Lake City | Charleston | Santa Fe | Santa Barbara

*For my grandmother, Myrtle Horst, who appreciates the beauty all around her
and understands the value of keeping a home filled with love.*

First Edition
12 11 10 09 08   5 4 3 2 1

Text © 2008 Kimberly Schlegel Whitman
Photographic credits on page 192

Published by
Gibbs Smith
P.O. Box 667
Layton, Utah 84041

Orders: 1.800.835.4993
www.gibbs-smith.com

Designed by m:GraphicDesign / Maralee Oleson
Printed and bound in China

Library of Congress Cataloging-in-Publication Data

Whitman, Kimberly Schlegel.
  Tablescapes : setting the table with style / Kimberly Schlegel Whitman. — 1st ed.
    p. cm.
  Includes bibliographical references and index.
  ISBN-13: 978-1-4236-0365-8 (alk. paper)
  ISBN-10: 1-4236-0365-6 (alk. paper)
  1. Table setting and decoration. 2. Entertaining. I. Title.
  TX879.W48 2008
  642´.6—dc22
                        2008009756

Acknowledgments

EVERY PROJECT TAKES A GREAT TEAM of people to complete. With this book the wonderful people who helped me out went above and beyond the call of duty working around my big pregnant belly! I owe a great deal of thanks to:

My patient and careful editor, Madge Baird, and the fantastic team at Gibbs Smith publisher, including Gibbs Smith, Christopher Robbins and Laura Ayrey.

My diligent manager, Gladys Gonzalez, and her team at John Carrabino Management; and my fantastic agents at ICM, Andrea Barzvi, Kimberly Oelman and Josie Freedman; Much & House Public Relations and Laura Ackerman, the hardest working gal in Los Angeles.

Photographers Scott Womack, Jason Wynn, Gary Donihoo and Stephen Karlisch.

Assistants without whose help I would not have survived: Misty McAfee, Candace Becker, David Garcia, Enrique Anguiano, Tom Vannoy, Eliza Powell, Valerie Osserman, Kimberly Zahniser, Suzy Harvey, Juana Maria Velezquez and Peter Bradbury.

Susan Spindler, who helped with almost every page of this book.

The vendors and venues that supplied their wares and made my tables come together: RSVP Soiree and Laurel Thomaschaske; Ducky Bob's; Suite 206 and Josh Madans; Chris Whanger for J&C Design; La Duni, Chuck Steelman and Neiman Marcus Willow Bend; Todd Fiscus, Christine Martin, Shelby Tomaso and Todd Events; Madison; Vivre; The Ritz-Carlton, Dallas; Hotel Crescent Court, Dallas; Frontiers of Flight Museum; Bella Flora; The Claridge; Porthault and Angela Malone; The Garden Gate Gifts and Florals; Needle in the Haystack; The Printery.

The talented calligraphers Laurie Harper, Boo Owens and Bernard Maisner.

The generous hostesses who took time out of their busy schedules to let us invade their homes and photograph their beautiful tabletop creations: Kelli Ford and Graham Lefford, Janet Rosell Rice, Peggy Sewell, Margaret Ryder and Gigi Lancaster, Natalie McGuire, Debbie Tolleson and Connie Howe.

My family, Kirby and Lauren, Kari, Krystal, Mom and Dad, Caroline, Stuart and Yulia, Kipp and Beth, Tony and Mary Ann, Scott and Lisa, Linda and Chris, Mike and Susan, my kind husband, Justin, and my precious son, JR. ❧

Contents

Family Style

Al Fresco

Introduction

MY FONDEST MEMORIES ARE OF TIMES SPENT around a table with friends and family. Whether for a casual family dinner or a large formal dinner party, the table is the perfect place to make new friends or catch up with old ones, try new cuisines or find comfort in classic recipes, share a recent joke or discuss the last book you read.

Whatever you do at your table, do it in style. With a little imagination, you can celebrate at every meal. Go the extra step to set a beautiful table, making memories for yourself, your friends and your family. This book shares some fabulous settings for family meals as well as ideas and inspirations for special-occasion tabletop designs. You will gain insight into tricks of the trade and ways to turn your tables into conversation starters.

Setting the table can be a family activity that enriches our daily lives. The time and care put into setting a table for family or guests is an expression of love. Details such as a beautiful napkin fold or a handwritten place card show that we care. The things that happen at the meal table affect our everyday moods and attitudes. Prayers, conversations and the rituals of dining are all things that play a role in our memories or recollections of a certain occasion. A meal can set the tone for the remainder of the day or evening, so it is important to make it beautiful. A well-designed table is a way to break the ice for guests who might not know how to start a new conversation, and—let's be honest—a well-designed table makes the food taste better!

Why do we set the table?

The purpose of entertaining is to have a good time and escape the woes and worries of everyday life. Gathering together with friends and family is the perfect form of stress relief. For me, setting the table is a therapeutic act. I forget about every other task that is on my "to do" list and focus on transforming the blank slate before me into a work of art. This is a quick and easy creative outlet that I get to practice every day! Some people find their creative escape in painting, drawing or sculpture. I find mine in setting the scene for a party.

Setting the table is really setting the stage for your meal. The meal is meant to be savored and enjoyed, so what is the point of preparing a wonderful meal or even taking the time to sit down at the table if you are not going to take the time to make the table attractive? The table setting should reflect the formality level and theme for your meal. This book includes every type of table setting, from a tray for a breakfast in bed to a long table for a formal celebration. I hope the ideas here will inspire you to set your table with style . . . even if it's just for your child's macaroni and cheese dinner!

Why is etiquette important?

Table etiquette is important even in today's lifestyle of fast-paced meals and racing out the door because it helps us feel confident in social situations. When we know what is expected of us, we can do it and know we are doing the right thing. There is nothing that can make us feel more uncomfortable than not knowing what to do when others are around. When we use our manners on an everyday basis, then going out to a restaurant or to a friend or colleague's home is not intimidating; it is just like any other meal. Table manners become automatic responses when we use them every day. When we can stop worrying about which fork to use, we are able to start focusing on enjoying our time with friends or making new acquaintances. What we learn and do at home goes with us when we dine elsewhere.

Even though some of the rules of etiquette seem silly, there is a reason behind each and every one of them. Most of them were created so that our experience at the table would be more pleasant.

For example, we are expected to motion our soupspoon away from us so that we do not spill or splash soup on ourselves. It makes sense when you start to think about the "why" behind the rule.

If you want to learn more about table etiquette, check out the huge selection of books on the subject. I love to browse through vintage ones at secondhand bookstores because the out-of-date situations can be comical. Still, the older books address many situations that arise today.

When in doubt as to how to behave at the table, always be gracious and polite. The worst thing you can do is to be rude or make someone else feel bad; so, if you need to break a rule in order to avoid hurting someone else, then do it!

How to be a great guest

Being a great guest is really quite simple: put yourself in the shoes (high heels, probably!) of the hostess and ask yourself what you can do to make her job easier. A few simple guidelines follow:

* Always reply promptly to your invitation. A hostess needs time to prepare, so let her know as soon as you know if you can attend. If you must decline an invitation, be sure to say why instead of leaving your hostess wondering. It is perfectly acceptable to say that you have already accepted another invitation or that you will be traveling. It is *not* acceptable to cancel an invitation you have previously accepted because you want to attend another event instead.

* Before you go, brush up on your knowledge of basic table manners and etiquette. For example, if you need to review your rule book to remember that your bread plate is on the left and your drinks are on the right, then do so.

* Be kind to everyone at the table, even if there is someone there that you don't get along with. The evening is not about you. It is about everyone having a good time.

* Keep the conversation going and flowing. Be sure to contribute to the conversation without monopolizing it. With people you are not very familiar with, you should probably avoid controversial subjects such as politics and gossip.

* For a seated dinner, a guest should arrive within fifteen minutes of the time on the invitation. Do not be early, though. Your hostess needs every moment she has to complete her last-minute tasks.

* Dress the part! Always dress for a party as the hostess requests.

* Never ever move a place card from where the hostess puts it. Every hostess puts a lot of thought into placing people at her party to stimulate good conversation, and you should honor her by accepting your seat graciously. If you really feel that you must be moved, discreetly approach the hostess during the cocktail hour and ask her to switch your seat. Do not do this as people are taking their seats.

* Remember that the goal of your hostess is to show you a good time . . . so have one!. ❧

One Table for One Hundred

A REHEARSAL DINNER IS AN IMPORTANT EVENT for any bride and groom, and especially for a mother of the groom, who is traditionally in charge of this celebration. I am lucky to have the chic, stylish and elegant Caroline Whitman as my mother-in-law. She had beautiful ideas for our rehearsal dinner and wanted to make it a night no one would ever forget.

Facing the challenge of providing an intimate evening dinner for over seventy-five members of the wedding party and their dates, with an ambiance that would be perfect for toasting, would have made most women run for cover. But not Caroline—she dove headfirst into making her plans while on a visit to Dallas from her hometown of Paris.

Step one was finding a location. Caroline opted to host the dinner in a tent, as she was trying to create a setting that was cozy as well as elegant and ethereal. A beautiful white tent erected on a tennis court provided the perfect spot for one gigantic table to seat 126 people. The table was made of platform staging in the center with 8-foot-by-30-inch tables placed all around the edge. The staging provided a strong and solid base for the centerpieces, while the tables provided a clean and comfortable place for the guests' place settings.

Caroline turned to the talented floral team from Dallas's Bella Flora to help make the center of the table perfect. For such a massive space, she wanted a lot of drama without it feeling too overwhelming.

The goal was to have a centerpiece that was both a conversation piece and an ethereal complement to the evening's activities. The solution was to assemble a collection of large-scale blue-and-white containers, clear glass vases and Lucite museum stands; we borrowed from friends, family and our favorite florists. To make pieces look even more substantial, some were inside Lucite boxes, some on top of high Lucite stands and others on top of small Lucite bases. Some containers were left empty and simply placed (along with their lids) in the center of the table; others were filled with yellow flowers. Large branches with yellow blooms and potted yellow tulips added life to the massive white setting. Large glass hurricanes and vases filled with yellow lemons added more color and captivating variety. Hundreds of small glass votive candles placed around the table added to the magical effect of the evening. The end result was a table of massive proportions that dazzled everyone who walked into the tent—perfect in its simplicity but dramatic in its scale.

The dinner was served to perfection by a team from Neiman Marcus, Caroline's favorite spot to lunch (and shop, of course) when she is in Dallas. She knew immediately that they had to cater the dinner that night, and they stepped up to the plate with grace and professionalism. The dinner was served on simple but high-quality white plates that were placed on woven wicker chargers. The chargers were an important element, as they framed the white plates against the background of the white table linen. Crisp and clean hemstitched white linen napkins sat on top of the plates, waiting to be placed on guests' laps.

Music During Dinner

Music is an essential part of any party. It is important that you plan ahead and prepare to have music that will enhance your celebration, instead of distract from it. This is especially important during a seated dinner. Personally, I like to play music that people will recognize because it helps them feel at home and at ease. Sometimes the music has lyrics; other times it's all instrumental.

Many hostesses firmly believe that music with lyrics distracts from conversation, but I have never found that to be a problem. For parties at home, I ask my husband to make a mix on his iPod of music appropriate to our dinner's theme. For example, if we are serving Italian food, he puts together a mix of songs from old Italian arias to Dean Martin.

For larger and more formal gatherings, it is a nice touch to hire a musician to provide live music. I love the harp, guitar or piano for these occasions. Be sure to help your musician prepare in advance for the type of music you want. I like to provide two lists: songs I would like to have played and songs I would like to avoid!

Each guest found his or her name in white ink on a blue place card. The menu, printed in blue on clean white paper, was placed in the center of each white plate. Silverware from Tiffany & Co. framed the plates to perfection, and beautiful but simple swirl stem crystal complemented the settings.

The overall look was better than any of us could have imagined, but the most memorable part of the evening came as the toasts were winding down to a close. When it was the groom's turn to make his toast, he carefully and unexpectedly pushed his place setting to the side and hopped up onto his chair and then onto the table! The space between the centerpieces and the place setting formed the perfect walkway for Justin to make his way around the table and tell each person there how grateful he was to have them in our lives. He stopped in front of his parents and said a few special words, then he thanked my parents and, finally, got down on his knee in front of where I was sitting and said the kindest words any bride could wish for from her groom. It was a perfectly magical moment that I will never forget and it took place on one of the most beautiful tables I could ever dream of. ❧

Love Bird Engagement Dinner

WHEN LOVE IS IN THE AIR, those around always want to celebrate. Justin and I were delighted when our dear friends Sheri and Bobby Staten offered to host a dinner in honor of our engagement. Sheri jumped into the party planning with zeal and delight. Bobby is a passionate wine collector, so he began selecting wonderful food and wines.

Because they knew it was my passion, the décor was left to me. The grand table required to accommodate eighty people needed a custom tablecloth. Sheri and I came up with a theme for the evening when I found pale blue fabric covered in beautiful birds. I loved the fabric the moment I saw it because not only were Justin and I affectionately referred to as "love birds," but also Sheri was a collector of antique birdcages; so the theme was perfect for both families involved. Countless yards of the beautiful fabric were purchased and sent off to the tailor to make a tablecloth.

We chose the Garden Room at the Hotel Crescent Court as the perfect venue for our grand dinner. The room's beautiful architecture and décor perfectly complemented our theme and colors, and their talented event planners and chefs accommodated all of Sheri and Bobby's special requests.

After cocktails on the adjacent terrace, the guests moved inside, where the dramatic table was

laid with the gorgeous tablecloth decorated with Sheri's lovely collection of antique birdcages. Our talented friend Sandy Krueger filled the bases of the birdcages with elegant blue hydrangeas and coral roses. Small French porcelain cachepots filled with flowers served as stands to give the birdcages height.

Wicker chargers held the menu cards and ivory hemstitched napkins. Guests were welcomed at their seats by a tiny nest holding little eggs and a card with their name and a personal message from Sheri in her signature penmanship. Exceptional wine, superb food and great friends were brought together with this beautiful setting. It was a night that Justin and I will never forget. ❦

Napkins

I am often asked for little lessons on napkins . . . where do they go? How do I use them? What color should they be? I always answer that there are simple rules that can be followed but that they are also meant to be broken! The perfect example of this is a story that my friend Paul Nicoli told me about one of his dinner parties. Paul and his partner, Jean Yves Ollivier, host some of the most beautiful and elaborate dinner parties at their homes in Paris, Morocco, Cape Town and the South African bush. The table is always set with wonderful centerpieces and elaborate china that Paul hunts for on his travels all over the world. On one occasion, Paul and his staff had forgotten to set the napkins on the table. He did not notice until all of his guests had been seated and everyone seemed to be looking around for their napkins. Paul thought quickly and asked one of the evening's servers to bring the napkins out on a silver tray and place one in each guest's lap. In the meantime, Paul made up a quick little story about how Napoleon liked his table service done this way, and his guests were enchanted! It was not until much later that he fessed up and told them the truth. It was a fun and memorable mistake that his guests have never forgotten! But if you are interested in knowing the rules, I have put together a little list that will hopefully help:

- After you have taken your seat at the table, place your napkin on your lap only after the hostess has done so. She may want to bless the food or say grace before the napkins are removed from the table, so wait for her to give you the cue.

- When placed on your lap, your napkin should be folded over by about one third of its size. Fold it neatly back toward your knees and it should be a perfect fit!

- Except to clean your mouth or a small spill, your napkin should remain in your lap the entire time you are seated.

- Your hostess will give you a cue that dinner is finished and that it is time to get up from the table when she puts her napkin on the table to the left of her plate. You will know that it is time to do the same!

- When you are getting up to excuse yourself from the table, place your napkin on the table to the left of your plate. You should not refold the napkin, but instead gather it up from the center and neatly place it there.

Grand Dining for a Governor

WHEN THE OPPORTUNITY TO ENTERTAIN ON A GRAND SCALE STRIKES, my mother seizes it and runs! She loves preparing for these special occasions. One such evening presented itself when my parents were asked to entertain California's Governor Arnold Schwarzenegger in their home while he was visiting in Texas. Where does one start to prepare for an event like this? We began by calling on our friend Todd Fiscus of Todd Events.

Although my parents have a large table in their dining room, accommodating thirty-six for a seated dinner required an alternative location. They had all of the furniture moved out of their formal living room and placed in storage, and then brought in large rental tables that were placed together as one long table down the middle of the room.

We used the custom gold pleated silk tablecloths with a black ribbon border from my wedding to Justin. Vintage gold Fortuny overlays with a black border, also from our wedding, were placed on top. To offset the traditional look of the room and the fabric, we used ultramodern apple green florals in both modern and traditional containers. Lucite squares with a beveled edge made the vases appear grander and anchored their visual presence on the table. Groups of nine small candles placed on smaller Lucite squares rendered an elegant glow.

Chivari chairs are available for rent in many colors from most party rental companies. In this case, black was the perfect complement to our tablecloths. The classic shape of the chairs and the modern glossy black paint complemented our classic-meets-modern look very well.

Sterling Christofle chargers at each setting were framed by beautifully polished silver bead flatware. Simple silver chalices for water tucked in between Waterford Lismore crystal wine glasses added sparkle to the table. The effect was stunning and dramatic. With so many place settings and such a long table, it was imperative that every plate and glass was set perfectly. For this formal affair, a ruler was used to measure the distance between pieces and make sure they were evenly set. The symmetry combined with the distance and repetition made a table that was attractive instead of cluttered. ❧

Lucite Bases

Lucite bases (see photo on page 22) make wonderful additions to any entertaining closet. They are elegant and chic, modern and classic at the same time. They can be used on the tabletop to raise the heights and the grandeur of candlesticks or floral containers. They can also be used in the foyer to frame a seating chart or escort cards. They are handy on a bar cart to hold the ingredients to a signature drink or as a serving tray (if the piece is thin and not too heavy) for hors d'oeuvres. Their clear surfaces can be quite delicate, so be careful not to scratch them with sharp objects; otherwise, use your imagination and have fun with them. I guarantee that you will use them repeatedly and they will become one of your favorite entertaining tools.

Off—Limit Spaces

On many occasions when entertaining in your home, your children will be upstairs doing homework or you will simply want privacy in certain areas of the house. When faced with the dilemma of politely informing your guests that the second story of your home is "off limits," a hostess can be creative. I hate the look of a velvet rope across the staircase and much prefer placing floral arrangements, flower petals and beaucoups votive candles on the stairs. Your point will be made but it will be made with style and beauty instead of intimidation.

DIGGING IN . . .

The hostess is the one who designates when it is time to eat. She marks the beginning of each course by picking up the appropriate utensils and starting to eat. If another guest is unaware of this rule of etiquette and starts to eat before the hostess does, the hostess should begin right away to save the guest embarrassment.

Love Is in the Air

W HEN MY DEAR FRIEND SUMMERLEE STATEN WAS PROPOSED TO in a biplane by her romantic beau, Brendan Rowe, we immediately knew what type of engagement party they needed. Everything about the dinner that my family hosted to honor their engagement was a nod to Brendan's love of aviation and his service in the air force. If we could have, we would have served the meal in the air!

Dallas's Frontiers of Flight Museum was the perfect spot for our aviation-themed formal dinner. This grand hangar has beautiful examples of some of history's most elegant airplanes, including a biplane that looked just like the one in which Brendan proposed to Summerlee. That airplane was red, so our color choices for the evening were easy.

When it came to setting up a table that would seat 110 people, we turned to our talented friend Todd Fiscus of Todd Events. He came up with a table scheme that resembled the shape of an airplane and accommodated our large guest list. It also had a wonderful head table attached, where the engagement party could be seated for convenient toasts to the future bride and groom.

By assembling a big group of rectangular rental tables, we created the table. A long spine down the center made the fuselage, with tail wings coming out at the end and a larger set of wings coming out near the center. All of these were covered in black satin cloths, while another long set of tables covered in silver satin cloths made up the propeller, which served as the head table. It was grand in scale and was a jaw-dropping sight.

Red chivari chairs with black cushions made a bold statement, but the most beautiful element of the table setting were the large cut-crystal containers holding masses of red roses. Candles of various heights added a romantic light and lit the florals from underneath, giving them a magical glow. Each place was marked with a place card created from a red leather luggage tag. The luggage tag also contained a "save the date" for the upcoming nuptials that would take place in Nashville six months later. They were the perfect party favor, too!

After the guests had mingled for about half an hour in the foyer of the museum, they were ushered into the main room of the museum's hangar where the wall was opened up for guests to witness the arrival of the guests of honor by private plane! It was a fun moment for all as the beautiful young couple descended from the steps of the plane to find more than a hundred of their closest friends and family lined up to celebrate with them. After all of the hellos and hugs were shared, the wall was closed up and dinner was served. A beautiful evening of toasts (and a few unscheduled roasts) and a delicious meal were proof that our efforts to make a special evening for this eclectic couple would not be forgotten. Creativity, thinking outside the box and stretching your imagination always make for a more memorable celebration. ❧

Chivari Chairs

Chivari chairs are one of my favorite solutions to table-setting dilemmas. They can be rented in many different colors and because they are quite narrow, you can squeeze more people in! They are also relatively inexpensive to purchase. Invest in some and paint them in your favorite fun color.

Family Tree
Anniversary Celebration

ONE OF THE GREAT BLESSINGS IN MY LIFE is my parents' happy and healthy marriage. They have always provided such a wonderful and loving home for my siblings and me, and we are so grateful. My mom is the glue that holds everything together, and when their thirty-fifth wedding anniversary came around, my father wanted to celebrate her! He had a great surprise up his sleeve and pulled off the most beautiful dinner with great flair.

The night before my parents' actual anniversary, my father invited his family and thirty-five friends to the Ritz Carlton Hotel for a surprise seated dinner and dancing. The décor and theme for the evening were based on the family tree. My parents both come from a long line of happy marriages and Dad wanted to celebrate that. As my mother is the one who typically gets everything together for these dinner parties, Dad knew he would need a little bit of help! We turned to the experts at Todd Events and they helped us turn the Ritz Carlton ballroom into an intimate forest for the family celebration.

Models dressed in copies of my mother's bridesmaids' gowns greeted the guests and directed them to an easel where they could sign a portrait of my parents with their original wedding party. Replicas of the bridesmaids' bouquets served as floral arrangements on the cocktail tables.

After the cocktail hour, which was complete with a selection of love songs from the year of their wedding, my parents led the guests into the dining room. My father had envisioned one long table for all of the guests, and in order to incorporate the family tree theme into the tablescape, we placed a real tree in the center of the table, beautifully lighted. At each end of the table, a TV monitor flashed a slideshow of my parents' wedding photos. The dramatic effect was mesmerizing, and it took us a long time get them seated, as they were all conversing about the table! Beautiful silver candelabras decorated with trees were filled with red roses and placed down the center of the table. The effect was lovely and opulent.

Rosenthal chargers in fall colors were set with artfully folded, hemstitched ivory linens bearing my parents' combined monogram.

Each guest's seat was designated by a place card written by the incredible Bernard Maisner of New York, a most gifted calligrapher who makes each word he writes into a piece of art. Many guests picked up their place cards at the end of the night and took them home as mementos! Next to the place cards were real leaves taken off the centerpiece tree. A menu card, also designed by Maisner, was tucked under each folded napkin.

As dinner progressed, my eloquent father made a toast, not only to his wife of thirty-five years, but also to every guest at the table, explaining why they were so special. In return, when we opened up the floor for toasts, many of the guests said a few words about my parents. After the main course was served, my parents cut the wedding cake and danced their "first dance." Guests flowed onto the dance floor in a lovely celebration of my parents' thirty-five years together.

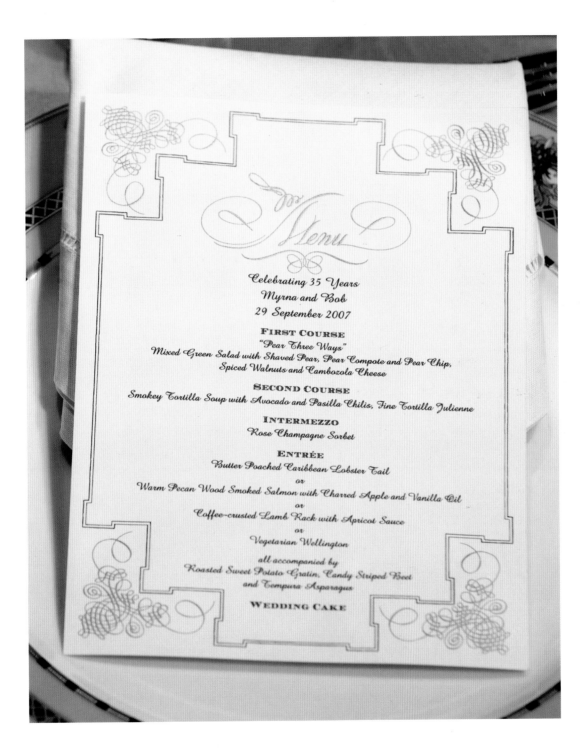

Menu

Celebrating 35 Years
Myrna and Bob
29 September 2007

FIRST COURSE
"Pear Three Ways"
Mixed Green Salad with Shaved Pear, Pear Compote and Pear Chip,
Spiced Walnuts and Cambozola Cheese

SECOND COURSE
Smokey Tortilla Soup with Avocado and Pasilla Chilis, Fine Tortilla Julienne

INTERMEZZO
Rose Champagne Sorbet

ENTRÉE
Butter Poached Caribbean Lobster Tail
or
Warm Pecan Wood Smoked Salmon with Charred Apple and Vanilla Oil
or
Coffee-crusted Lamb Rack with Apricot Sauce
or
Vegetarian Wellington

all accompanied by
Roasted Sweet Potato Gratin, Candy Striped Beet
and Tempura Asparagus

WEDDING CAKE

Baby Shower in Blue and Pink

CELEBRATING THE IMPENDING ARRIVAL of a new baby is the most fun and inspiring celebration of all. For my friend Janet Rosell Rice, I felt especially inspired. Janet is a stylist for lifestyle and design magazines and was pregnant with her first child. Because she and her husband decided to be surprised about the sex of the baby, we celebrated the possibilities with a blue and pink luncheon for twelve of Janet's closest friends.

I adore blue and white anything! It is such a fresh and pretty color combination. Add in some pink and our shower theme was born. A white linen tablecloth from Porthault gave my dark wood dining table a bright look, perfect for a luncheon. My dining table is an odd size—long and narrow—so I had Porthault make this cloth to measure. A crisp and simple high-quality white linen tablecloth should be in every household. It is the perfect backdrop for any table setting. In the center of the table, I gathered together my collection of blue-and-white containers in various sizes. Various shades of pink roses added depth to the floral arrangements and were the perfect way to tie in the "little girl factor."

I placed two wooden figurines in the center of the table—a young girl and a young boy—gifts from my mother-in-law from a Paris flea market.

Every element needed to fit the color scheme, right down to the place cards, which were a bold blue embellished with pink ink. Pink linen napkins with my monogram in white perfectly pulled the color from the center of the table to the fun and colorful place settings; I was thrilled for the opportunity to mix and match some of my favorite patterns. A beautiful blue-and-white Mottehedah charger was the perfect frame for my favorite china pattern, Mottehedah's "Tobacco Leaf," a gift from my mother, which was used as the service plate. I always like to have a plate that is full of color placed at each setting so that when guests arrive at their seats, their setting looks complete even without food. Just before the first course is served, the servers come around and collect the service plate but leave the charger. The plated second course is placed on the charger.

The menu at this baby shower was inspired by the cravings of the pregnant guest of honor. Her biggest craving was carrots, so carrot soup was our delicious first course. It was served in a pink-and-white bowl from a vintage set that I purchased years ago at an estate sale. The markings on the service are Portuguese and I don't think the set is very "important," but I love it! Our second course, a delicious chicken salad, was served on the "Tobacco Leaf" plates. For dessert, our delicious fruit salad was served on the pink-and-white set again.

This luncheon also gave me an opportunity to show off the Puiforcat silver that my mother-in-law gave Justin and me as a wedding gift. It was the silver that she received when she married Justin's father. It is engraved with the most exquisite W monogram and each piece is so beautiful. I was thrilled to be able to use it on such a special occasion.

Only the best would do for this formal luncheon, so my favorite stemware came out of the closet, too. The "Printemps" pattern from Varga is a perfect daytime delight, with its lovely colors and cheerful etchings. I used the pink and blue and mixed in a little bit of yellow, too. I left the green stemware in the cupboard. Even though the guest of honor could not indulge, I wanted to serve wine and champagne to mark this miraculous occasion. After salad and dessert courses, we moved from the dining room into the living room, where Janet was showered with her gifts. It was a beautiful afternoon with a table to suit. ❧

Pour Memoir Cards

I love the process of putting together a dinner party for six or eight people. Each host has a different number that works for her; for me, eight is enough for a seated dinner. My favorite way to extend an invitation for a dinner party, especially one of that size, is to call. The telephone is the perfect way to reach out and ask someone to join you. Once they accept your invitation, you can ask another couple who would mix well with the group you are forming and so on and so on. You can customize your guest list and put together a dinner party with chemistry this way. It is important, I believe, to follow up with a Pour Memoir, or To Remind, card. You can either find a lovely blank card and ask your calligrapher to write it out for you or you can have some printed with your name and spaces to fill in. The verbiage should go like this:

To Remind
Mr. and Mrs. Justin Whitman
are expecting
Insert guest's name
for dinner *(lunch, brunch, etc.)*
at *insert time here*
insert address

Christmas with Tiffany's

THE CHRISTMAS HOLIDAYS ARE THE MOST MAGICAL time of year. I adore the scents of balsam and peppermint, the colors of the decorations popping up all around, the sounds of the carols and the sight of the lights on our neighbors' homes as we drive around in the evening. It is a time of year that fills people with a spirit of generosity and giving and, therefore, is an especially wonderful time of year to entertain.

Get-togethers with friends and family should be stepped up a notch from regular parties and celebrated with abandon during all holidays, but especially Christmas. This was always the case with my mother's formal Christmas celebrations. My mother has been collecting Tiffany's holiday china for many years and loves to pull it out for her Christmas celebrations. The china is covered in beautiful red ribbons, gold accents,

acorns and pine needles. Setting up a table in the "Red Room" at their home has become a much-anticipated event.

This particular occasion called for a round table set for eight people. As this room is not typically meant for dining, we had to move furniture around and bring in a 66-inch round table to set underneath the beautiful Baccarat chandelier. The table was covered with an iridescent red and green cloth that was custom-made several years ago for my party rental company, RSVP Soiree. I have since sold this business but I still call there often for rentals! This occasion was the perfect time to bring out this cloth again, as it had always been the perfect companion for the beautiful holiday china.

The center of the table was set with a mirrored tray with a bronze doré trim. The formal and elaborate tray usually resides on the dining room table in the shape of an oval, but we took off the two ends and placed them together to make a circle perfect for this round table. The mirrored tray set the centerpiece of holiday greens and red roses apart from the rest of the table. Designer Susan Spindler arranged the flowers in an etched crystal bowl with a bronze edge by Moser. To fill in the additional space on the mirrored tray, we gathered small gold-leaf dishes from William Yeoward and charming little Baccarat angels. Additional holiday greenery was placed around the base of the tray and small balsam tea lights were mixed in.

Each place was set with an ornate gold charger from Faberge and dinner and salad plates from Tiffany's. The ornate glassware from Moser was covered in the same etching as on the centerpiece's container. The glasses had an additional, special, personalized touch, as my mother had them custom-made and monogrammed with a gold "S." Gold flatware complemented the formality of the rest of the setting. Salt cellars with angels were placed at each setting, as well as a napkin elaborately embroidered with red and green poinsettias.

As the finishing touch, chairs from the dining room were set up around the table after the table was laid. Their dark ebonized wood added a rich finish to the table. (Always set the table before you bring the chairs up to it as they block your access.) Setting the table with style, care and attention to details is one of the greatest gifts that you can give—so celebrate the holidays with your greatest tabletop ideas. ❧

SEATING ARRANGEMENTS

Seating arrangements for formal dinner parties are very important and should be laid out with careful consideration for the experience your guests will have. A seating arrangement can change a guest's life! You never know what might happen at a dinner party. When making your seating arrangement, always have the host at the head of the table. Place yourself, as the hostess, at the opposite end of the table, with easy access to the kitchen if necessary. A female guest of honor should be placed to the right of the host and a male guest of honor should be placed to the right of the hostess. (If you are hosting a ladies' luncheon, the guest of honor should be seated across from the hostess.) The only other rule of thumb that is much appreciated is the idea that an engaged couple should not be split up. This rule should be honored until the newlyweds have reached their one-year wedding anniversary. Beyond these simple guidelines, you can seat the rest of the guests as you wish. A pattern of male/female/male is usually best for a coed guest list.

Easter Dinner

ASTER DINNER IS A SPECIAL TIME for families to gather together and celebrate. My mother is a pro at making every day feel like a holiday, but she especially loves Easter. She is famous for her weekend breakfast "dippy eggs" and has been collecting antique silver eggcups for many years. Her expansive collection usually adorns the side buffet table in her dining room. Over the years, it has grown so large that many of her beautiful pieces get stored away, but when Easter approached this particular year, we decided to pull them out and allow them to shine as they were originally meant to—on the table.

We used the silver eggcups as decoration down the center of the very large dining room table, which seats twenty-two people. Spreading these small but charming items across the center of the table allowed everyone to see clearly. We filled the eggcups with pastel-colored eggs and added Easter lilies in small mint julep cups for a touch of life.

My mother has never hesitated to use her most precious china even for simple family dinners, and the Easter table was no exception. She brought out her collection of beautiful Fabergé "Egg" china. This pattern isn't used often, but it always draws "oohs" and "ahhhs" when it is set out. A white linen tablecloth was the perfect backdrop for all of these precious things. White linen napkins embroidered with lily of the valley, another treasured Easter flower, adorned each place setting. These napkins were specially created by purchasing lovely but simple plain white linen napkins and providing lily of the valley artwork to a monogram shop. They gave us a book of thread colors

to choose from and then embroidered our favorite flower onto the napkins. These little touches are the things that make setting the table magical. It is such a treat to fold and place a tabletop item that was born in your imagination!

Sterling silver flatware was placed at each setting. A beautiful set of antique mother-of-pearl-handled knives was mixed in as well. Mixing silver flatware patterns adds interest to the table and breaks up the monotony of the flatware.

I have learned a lot of things from my mother over the years, but I especially appreciate that she taught me to seize each moment with family and friends and always use the best things you have available to you. Easter is a time of gratitude and a day when we put on our best dresses and suits. We should dress our tables up in their Easter best as well! ❧

MONOGRAMS

Find a monogram shop that you like and take in some of your simple and plain napkins. On linens, either one letter (from your surname) or the hostess's monogram should be used. For example, our napkins have either a W or KSW on them. Some people like to combine the husband's and wife's names into one monogram (jWk in our case), but this is not the traditional format. Of course, you can make an exception to this rule if you are celebrating a gentleman's birthday and would like to monogram his initials and give the linens to him as a gift afterward.

Silver Eggcups

Silver eggcups were a favorite of the Victorians, who took the art of dining very seriously. As a result, many new service items were created for the table during this time, and silversmiths, exploiting their new prosperity, began offering new designs and styles with uses that were as specific as possible. The covered egg coddler was designed to keep the eggs warm at the table. The toast racks were designed to display the toast in a lovely symmetrical way, and many of the eggcups have special spoons supported nearby. I especially love the individual one pictured here that is designed like a rack being carted around by a little angel. The wheels actually turn and this beautiful service piece can be moved around the table. The sweetheart egg rack (see page 60) is perfect for a romantic breakfast in bed. Most of the egg racks pictured here date from 1860 to 1910.

Thanksgiving Reflections

*T*HANKSGIVING IS A TIME FOR REFLECTION: it is a time to sit back and think about all of the blessings we have to be thankful for. When I set my Thanksgiving table, I like to take this idea of reflection literally and use soft, shiny, reflective surfaces that are a more modern twist on the traditional Thanksgiving table. Using a mirrored tabletop is a youthful and fun tradition that any family could incorporate into their setting. Mirrored tabletops can be purchased or rented. They are made in many shapes and sizes and I chose to use a square this year. To complement the mirrored top, I chose a geometric silver fabric for the tablecloth. I also rented silver chairs to replace my wood and leather chairs so that the chairs would go along with the look of the table. The mirror looked especially pretty in my dining room as it complemented my silver Gracie wallpaper.

In the center of the table I made a big pile of gourds and corn that had been spray painted silver. I mixed in red votive candles to give the table a touch of color that was slightly different from the typical harvest color scheme. Red glass chargers were placed at each seat to bring more color to the table; they were the perfect backdrop for my collection of black-and-white turkey plates and red glass turkey soup tureens.

Silver flatware decorated with pheasants and white linen monogrammed napkins were placed formally at each seat. Everything on the table glistened, even the place cards, which were hand-painted black and red on reflective silver paper.

Personal mementos are the things that make a table special, and this table setting included several of them. The beautiful silver chalices set for water at each place setting have been collected by family members over the years to mark special occasions. They are each monogrammed with a message and a date, and it is

always fun to read each one and be reminded of that wonderful birthday or anniversary. Small silver birds—party favors from our wedding—were placed on the sideboard. Buccellati silver leaves that Justin and I purchased together on a vacation were placed around the table as decorations and to hold breads and salts. Each item brought a smile to my face as I placed it on the table and reminisced about where it came from. ❧

Simple Sophistication

WE HAVE ALL BEEN TOLD AT ONE POINT IN OUR LIVES TO "KEEP IT SIMPLE." I think this little bit of advice can certainly apply to the table as well. Too many times I find myself overloading a tabletop with things that disrupt the harmony and balance that the table should have. In setting this table for a formal dinner for six, I had to really exercise restraint—not an easy thing for me.

My inspiration for the table came from the Robert Motherwell painting hanging by the dining table. My goal was to bring out the blue in the simple Abstract Expressionist painting with beautiful blue hydrangeas that were just at the peak of their season. I placed the hydrangeas in white porcelain urns that my husband and I found on one of our frequent Saturday afternoon antiquing excursions. Between the two white urns I placed a pair of small bronze-capped urns that we found at the Paris flea market. I resisted my usual urge to place small containers of white flowers all around the blank spaces in the center of the table, and I believe the table looked better for it.

When you are keeping it simple, as I was here, it is very important to use the highest quality. I did that here with my favorite place mats and napkins from Porthault. The linen is exquisite and the embroidery around this complicated edge was all done by hand. It was almost frightening to serve food near it! I also used beautiful blue antique Venetian glasses that were given to us as a very special wedding gift from our friend Donald Coan. They had belonged to his aunt and he generously passed them to us. I felt that they were too beautiful to stay in the cabinet, and this was the perfect setting for them.

Simple but beautiful china from Richard Ginori complemented the Porthault linens. The china had the same blue dots around the edge that the linens did. The chocolate brown-and-white landscape scene in the center of the plates added the touch of interest necessary to keep the table from being too simple.

Christofle's "Aria" gold silverware was a beautiful addition to our tabletop. The 1950s honey-colored table with a gorgeous glossy finish and the 1940s x-back chairs added the perfect amount of elegance. I could not wait for the guests to arrive to complete our table. ❧

Après Ski Supper

AFTER AN EXHILARATING BUT EXHAUSTING day on the slopes in Aspen, Colorado, Peggy Sewell likes to help her family's guests unwind with a little bit of wine and cheese served in the wine cellar. The ritual is done in great style, with Peggy's collection of antiques taking center stage.

The scene-stealer on this table is the collection of charming handwoven linens from the 1940s. Not only are they meticulously detailed and handcrafted, but they also have an interesting provenance: they were formerly part of the collection of the Baroness Rappasardi from her villa in Florence. These linens portray the story of the Hunting of the Unicorn that is based on the Bayreuth tapestries in the Metropolitan Museum of Art collection.

Other antique details include beautiful ivory-handled flatware placed beside antique English Masons iron-stone plates, and a large wooden tray with bone handles, holding a smaller silver tray with an assortment of antique horn-handled cheese knives and serving pieces.

When supper is served, the Sewells and their guests gather at the table for a sumptuous meal. Again, Peggy's great style is highlighted through her collection of beautiful tabletop items. Atop a long and narrow wooden table, Peggy placed three floral arrangements (created by Aspen Branch), allowing for easy conversation across the table. The handpainted china is by Anna Weatherly and the purple glasses are by William Yeoward. Silver flatware from Ercuis is mixed with ivory-handled antique fish knives and forks.

To set the mood, Peggy recommends using large quantities of votives and tall tapers for soft light. Her table setting ensures that family and friends will enjoy nourishment and be ready for another day on the slopes. ❧

Butterfly Brunch

AYA ANGELOU HAS SAID THAT LOVE allows us to not only survive but to "thrive with passion, compassion and style." Designer Susan Spindler loves this thought, as it embodies what life and entertaining are all about. Susan is an eclectic designer who can style any event, from a formal dinner in a sleek and modern airplane hangar to an all-American Christmas in a traditional home.

Susan believes that any celebration, event or party feels special when attention is given to detail. This is certainly evident in her fantastic butterfly table setting. Her inspiration started with the beautiful butterflies, which she had spotted at a Neiman Marcus store, and everything on the table is connected to the theme. She started with the china, a handpainted set from Anna Weatherly, decorated with dainty flowers and butterflies. Beneath the plates, Susan set bold porcelain chargers, each in a different color, setting the china apart from the crisp white linen tablecloth.

Susan set the tone for this event by placing a beautiful arrangement of flowers in the center of the table that complemented the flowers portrayed on the china. She also mimicked the butterflies from the china in the floral arrangement by connecting silk butterflies to the ends of wires. Susan always likes a centerpiece to be low enough that it does not block the line of sight across the table.

Butterflies were also themed on the napkin rings, on the serving pieces set around the table and even in the beautiful Varga crystal wineglasses.

I love Susan's philosophy on entertaining. She says that "entertaining is a gift you give your guests from the moment they open their invitation to your welcoming them at your front door to the tone created at each table setting. You are setting the stage for a wonderful meal, conversation and gathering for friends, old and new." What a treat it is to be her guest! ✤

BUTTERFLY BRUNCH

Harvest Feast

Neighbors and lifelong friends Gigi Lancaster and Margaret Ryder are true connoisseurs of tabletop finery. They work well together because their strengths (Gigi's in linens, Margaret's in floral arranging) are complementary.

Together this duo set an elegant rustic table in front of a roaring fire to host an autumn supper. They creatively and effortlessly combined antique pewter, Gien Rambouillet china and Leontine Linens monogrammed napkins. They selected vintage sugar bowls to serve as wine glasses. Canadian pewter flatware in the shape of branches and wonderful candlesticks filled with beeswax taper candles were beautiful beside the monogrammed antique pewter charger plates. An artfully designed hydrangea bouquet was the perfect centerpiece.

The china, depicting endangered animal species, reflected their use of organic and natural elements while underscoring their love of animals and whimsy. This eclectic table also included bowls full of clementines, antique wine decanters and silver chalices decorated with hunting dogs. It flawlessly mixed candles, flowers, vintage collectibles, antique treasures and modern pieces to create a festive and comfortable atmosphere for guests. ❧

FORMAL DINING AT HOME

An Asian Evening

WHEN NATALIE MCGUIRE SETS OUT TO DO A PARTY, the sky is the limit. She does everything with style and great thought. So Justin and I felt honored that she and her husband, Mike, offered to give a party in honor of our upcoming nuptials.

Because so many of the events surrounding our marriage had been planned around my preferences, Natalie and Mike wanted this party to honor Justin's desires. She knew that Justin loves the color red and that he loves sushi—so she planned an indoor/outdoor Asian-themed party. Natalie enlisted the help of the talented Todd Fiscus to help with décor and flowers, and he did an incredible job. The modern and chic Asian-inspired flowers were a perfect complement to the beautiful buffet. Outdoors, hanging lanterns over the sushi bar and refreshment buffet provided perfect mood lighting.

Three buffet tables were set up around their lovely home, the largest being their formal dining room table, which held hot Asian dishes from George Catering. This was the perfect location, as its proximity to the kitchen made it easy for the catering staff to keep an eye on the table. A second buffet table, draped in red and white tablecloths, was set up outside. It held all sorts of sushi and was a very popular spot. A third buffet holding Asian drinks was lit from beneath, so the sakes and cocktails glowed.

It was a stunning and dramatic setup. As wonderful as the table-tops were, the highlight of the evening was the appearance of the McGuires' daughters, Madison and Sophie, who paraded around the party in beautiful Asian costumes with chopsticks in their hair!

Pampered Pink Spa Party

A GIRLS' NIGHT OUT is always fun, but a girls' night *in* can be even better! I was honored by my friends Connie Howe and Debbie Tolleson with a girls' night in before my wedding. The spa party had a Pampered Pink theme that Connie and Debbie took to the limits with this soiree, which was held at Debbie's home in a large party room that they literally transformed into a Pink Spa for my family and friends. They set up rooms for massage, had a station for manicures and pedicures, a spot to have hair and makeup done, as well as a table where an expert would read your colors! And we can't forget about the table—it was pink perfection that caught the eye of every guest as she walked in.

What made the party such a success was the attention to detail from start to finish. As guests arrived, they were greeted by Connie and Debbie dressed in fuzzy pink bathrobes. Each guest was handed a boat bag from L.L. Bean that had been monogrammed with their name and contained fuzzy pink robes monogrammed with "Pampered Pink" and personalized with their name, a pair of flip flops with Pampered Pink written in rhinestones, and a locker key so that each of the girls could change into their new spa wear and lock up their clothing.

After changing into their robes, the guests were escorted into the Spa Room, where they were given instructions for the afternoon. Step one was to help themselves to the magnificent buffet. The large rectangular table was a wonderland of all things pink and girlie. Magnificent fashion mannequins dressed in towels in every shade of pink were the highlight of the table. The towels were masterfully draped to make the mannequins look like they could have been found in the windows of Neiman Marcus. They were a jaw-dropping conversation piece—so much so that one almost missed the fact that there was food on the table!

Once you got a taste of it, though, the food was unforgettable. The beautiful presentation and delicious light foods were perfect for the ladies. Beautiful melons, individual pink Chinese food containers filled with fresh Asian chicken salad, and, of course, pink chocolate-covered strawberries were presented on beautiful trays. The tabletop was woven with runners in different shades of pink, and floral arrangements were set in silver high heels. Even the drinks went along with the theme: water bottles—a necessity at any spa—were covered in a stretchy, shiny fabric, trimmed with white feather boas and even monogrammed with the "pampered pink" theme. The talented hostesses spent an entire weekend decorating the glassware and stemware with pink hearts, rhinestones and flowers. Even the servers and spa therapists wore white coats monogrammed with "pampered pink" on the pockets.

This party was the pink of perfection! We were poofed and pumiced and pampered—and we truly loved every moment of it. ❖

PAMPERED PINK SPA PARTY

Pampered Pink Spa Party

Holiday Dessert Buffet

THE HOLIDAYS ARE SUCH A BUSY TIME OF YEAR. With so many people we want to celebrate with and so many items on our list of things to
do, it can become completely overwhelming. Another challenge: finding
an evening to have your party when people don't have another invitation! My
favorite solution to this problem is the always-popular dessert buffet, starting at
nine o'clock or later; if your recipients have a dinner obligation elsewhere, they can
always accept your "after party" invite to finish off their evening. Justin and I hosted
a fun and playful Christmas-candy-themed dessert buffet that was a hit.

Guests were greeted at the door by a server offering our evening's signature
drinks: frozen white chocolate concoctions that got people returning to the door for
seconds! The next sight for each guest was the dessert buffet set up in our formal
dining room. The table was covered with treats of every sort, from chocolate to
citrus, and it was truly a feast for the eyes. The desserts were served on silver and
crystal cake platters and trays and in dishes. Silver serving pieces were set up near
every dessert on small silver bread plates so there was a clean and convenient place
to set them down again. Frosted glass plates with silver bead decorations were set
out on the dining room buffet along with flatware and napkins so guests could help
themselves throughout the late evening.

I embellished the table with my collection of vintage Santa Claus figures and
Christmas trees. Regular floral arrangements just would not do in this case—they
would simply have gotten lost on the table as all eyes went to the sweets, so I added
old-fashioned holiday lollipops to the arrangements. The stems of the lollipops
were stuck right into the floral oasis just like the flower stems. And, of course, no
dessert buffet would be complete without a gingerbread house made of candy!

To top it all off, there was a candy buffet set up outside for our guests to
choose from to satisfy the next day's sweets cravings. Vintage Christmas candy
ribbons, Red Hots, red and green M&Ms, candy canes and, of course, Whitman's
Holiday Samplers, were placed in large glass containers for our guests to take home.
Small cellophane bags were set out and silver scoops were placed in each container
so guests could take a bag of sweets to remember their evening by. ❧

Father's Day

ON FATHER'S DAY, I AM OFTEN BAFFLED by the challenge of what I can do for my dad. He does so much for me, and I can't imagine that I will ever be able to say "thank you" properly. But at least I can plan a wonderful meal at a beautifully set table. Gathering around the table with his family seems to be one of my dad's favorite things to do.

It struck me one day that if we collected a big group of neckties, they would make a perfect overlay for a round table. A trip to the Salvation Army for an affordable tie collection did the trick. I presented the challenge to Nicolas Villalba, a Dallas couturier, who accepted with enthusiasm. He began with a large circle of solid fabric and tacked each of the ties down to make this fantastic and memorable overlay. Underneath, we made a tablecloth from gentlemen's suiting material, a wonderful black-and-white houndstooth pattern with blue accents. We had napkins made from dress shirt fabric and folded them to resemble a shirt pocket. "Aria" gold sterling from Christofle, with its tailored and refined masculine lines, was the flatware for this occasion. Solid beer steins in Tiffany and Co.'s Atlas collection stood in for the standard water glass, and modern china from Rosenthal carried through our masculine look.

The unusual challenge of setting the table for a man is that oftentimes flowers are not exactly their idea of a perfect centerpiece. Candles are always a nice alternative, and, in this case, I placed black tapers in classic silver candleholders free of any ornate pattern or floral design that could be interpreted as feminine. Small square bowls of M&Ms—my father's favorite candy—were

placed opposite the candleholders. I chose only black and white M&Ms, to accent the colors in the tablecloth. Topping off the table were gifts for each guest to commemorate the special occasion. The gifts were wrapped in another of my father's favorites—the business section of the *Wall Street Journal*.

The only thing left to do after the table was set was to gather around and toast the man of the day. My family loves to take turns around the table on these special occasions and say something meaningful about the guest of honor. And my father always likes to have the opportunity, after we have all spoken our tribute to him, to say something wonderful to each of the guests. That is one of the many qualities that make him the man we love to celebrate. ❧

Valentine's Day Tray

LTHOUGH I TRULY BELIEVE that every morning is cause enough for celebration and should begin with breakfast in bed, I understand that this is usually a rare treat. I can think of no more romantic excuse for treating your spouse to a beautiful breakfast tray than Valentine's Day. Porthault makes wonderful patterned trays that are perfect for such an occasion. For this Valentine's Day celebration I chose one in the pink hearts pattern and used a pink-and-white Porthault print place mat.

Coffee was served from a monogrammed coffeepot by Raynaud into a small, pink, heart-shaped coffee mug. Heart-shaped pancakes were served on a Porthault breakfast plate with a rim covered in pink hearts that match the tray. A small gift was wrapped in pink tulle and ribbon.

Only the finest will do for the ones we love, so I pulled out our best silver for this special occasion. Our flatware from Puiforcat, a gift from my husband's mother, is monogrammed with a beautiful W. A pink enamel antique napkin ring held the napkins—a pretty embroidered white one mixed with the pink-and-white napkin from the Porthault breakfast set. Every piece on the tray was intended to pamper my Valentine.

VALENTINE'S DAY TRAY

Breakfast in the Afternoon

FOR ME, SETTING THE TABLE IS A GREAT CREATIVE OUTLET. I take every opportunity, even a brunch with girlfriends in the breakfast room, to do just that. On one such occasion, I invited five friends for breakfast in the afternoon.

To set a ladylike tone, I began with a simple white cloth and a lily of the valley–patterned overlay from Porthault. This is a set we use nearly every day—a green-and-white plate with tiny green flowers that we brought home from a trip to Paris and a smaller breakfast plate from Porthault with a border of green clover. Ceramic bouquets of flowers from Christian Dior provided a special touch at each place setting; these bouquets were moved to the table when the food was served.

In the center of the table was a beautiful lemon topiary created by my friend Susan Spindler. Susan came over with a bag full of tools, I provided the lemons and off we went to create this long-lasting arrangement. Small pieces of hydrangea left over from another dinner party filled in the spaces and the topiary sprang to life.

We laid out cheerful silver flatware with an enchanting bird pattern and placed a vintage chick eggcup beside each juice glass. Informal place cards in green and white stripes marked the seating. To add to the garden feel, I brought outdoor chairs into the breakfast room. The refreshing view out the window and into the garden was the final perfect element and our breakfast in the afternoon was a relaxing time well spent.

Jadeite Dinner

I HAVE ALWAYS BEEN A COLLECTOR. As a child, I was fascinated with putting together the perfect sticker collection and doll collection. As I got older, I became obsessed with finding things for my tabletops. One of the things that caught my eye, long before Martha Stewart made them popular, were jadeite pieces from Fire King. Even as a student in my first apartment, I loved spending weekends scouring flea markets and garage sales looking for jadeite. My family knew of my passion for piecing together a set for my table and always kept an eye out as well. Piece by piece I assembled enough interesting plates and vases to host a dinner for eight.

I like to use my jadeite in a way that embraces the set's best feature—its color. The unusual jadeite green is not found many places, but I fell in love with a chinoiserie fabric in the perfect shade of green mixed with robin's egg blue. I love the unexpected color combination and the pale ivory background.

Our long ivory damask drapes provided the perfect backdrop to set up my table. A set of French chairs with green painted frames and ivory upholstery— normally set around our formal living room—made the perfect seating for my jadeite table. The chairs and tablecloth added a touch of formality to a dinner setting that was originally made for everyday use in the kitchen.

The napkins were a great find in the most perfect shade of robin's egg blue. I even found place cards in that wonderful color. I gave calligrapher Laurie Harper a swatch of our tablecloth fabric and she added our guests' names in the perfect shade of green ink. Waterford "Lismore" pattern crystal, from my mother's collection, added a bit of sparkle and pizzazz. The centerpiece for the table was made up of a variety of jadeite containers filled with flowers that were both fun and formal.

I wanted to show off all of my more interesting pieces so, during the coffee service, the cow-shaped creamer and old-fashioned sugar dispenser found their way to the table. The combination of formal and informal made our guests feel special but also kept them at ease—the perfect recipe for a dinner well set!

Jadeite Fire King

Jadeite Fire King was first made by the
Anchor Hocking Glassware Company in the
1940s. It was designed to be ovenproof in a
time when many kitchens across the country
were being updated with the latest technology
in ovens and other gadgets. The jadeite collection was not only durable and inexpensive but
also bold and attractive. It became Anchor
Hocking's most popular seller. Jadeite is fun to
collect, mix and match, and use both daily and
on special occasions. Be cautious when collecting Jadeite Fire King in today's market,
though, as its popularity has made it more
expensive and caused a flood of reproductions.

Nautical at Night

O N AN OVERCAST OR WINDY night at our lake house in Ontario, Canada, there is only one spot to eat—but it's a great one. A simple and elegant nautical theme is perfect in this house with its pine paneling and lighthouse towers. A large model sailboat, plucked from a shelf in the home library, served as the perfect focal point and suited the narrow Mennonite farm table perfectly. White and navy bowls filled with white dahlias accented the sailboat on each side.

Even though it might not be ideal weather for dining outdoors, we still like to have cocktails on the deck and listen to the waves roll in. Large dispensers filled with iced tea and lemonade are left out most evenings so that people are free to fill up their cups whenever they please.

Dining at the lake is a casual affair but that doesn't mean that the table doesn't deserve attention. My mother uses a different setting almost every night! My personal favorite is a vintage set; the dinner plates are decorated in navy blue with a logo from a cruise ship, and the salad plates have a small gold anchor logo in the center of the rim. The plates are placed on top of woven raffia place mats found at the Saturday market in St. Tropez, France. Mixed with navy and white geometric patterned napkins from Madison in Dallas, and life preserver napkin rings, they are the perfect touch.

Blue glassware looks wonderful on almost any summer table with any theme. Navy-handled flatware from Pottery Barn adds a touch of additional color to the natural palette beneath. Other nautical details can be found around the table. The place cards are embellished with a sailor's knot at the top. A silver monkey's fist knot and a vintage brass anchor decorate the table as well. Even the salt and pepper shakers are shaped like lighthouses. ⚓

Fairy-Tale Gnome Lunch

I FIND MY INSPIRATION FOR EACH table setting that I create in various things. I never know when I am going to find a figurine of a bird that will inspire an entire tabletop or a vase that will drive me to pull out a tablecloth that has been stuck in the back of the closet for a number of years. In this case, my inspiration came from a charming set of china that my parents brought back to me from a trip they took to Germany.

Pregnant with our first baby (and my parents' first grandchild), I was getting so much joy out of preparing for this new arrival. The china set was the perfect way to prepare our table for him. Each little plate, bowl, mug and coffeepot was handpainted with a different scene from a fairy tale. I found pleasure in studying each one and imagined planning a lunch for our little one and his friends in the garden. Even though he had not arrived on the scene yet, I decided to set the table in his honor and have lunch under our big oak tree. Each plate in the set featured a different fairy tale, but they all included woodland animals and little gnomes. To create the tablescape, my first call was to Suite 206, a Dallas-based party rental company specializing in chic furniture and other decorative event elements. They had exactly what I needed— a faux bois tree table! This most elaborate table for four had a tree trunk–shaped base. They also had funny gnome stools that were the perfect complement to our fairy-tale china.

My friend Susan Spindler and I covered the table in green moss instead of a tablecloth; a cloth would have covered the elaborate tree base, while the moss was a great way to carry out the fairy-tale theme. In the center of the table we placed a little birdhouse from Smith and Hawken. We

covered the birdhouse in Spanish moss to give it the look of the cottages depicted on the china. The final touch to the centerpiece was little woodland animal ornaments, also from Smith and Hawken. I cut the ornament hooks off the animals and placed them around the table. They looked just like the woodland animals in the china. Natural linen napkins were placed at each setting and tied with a gnome glass ornament that also served as the party favor.

Rain threatened to pour down the day of our lunch, so the table was moved inside and we opened the doors onto the garden instead. This was my first reminder that, especially when you throw children into the mix, things don't always go as planned!

The table was whimsical and fun and the child-like setting made it even more relaxing. I can't wait to re-create it for my son and his friends when he's old enough to enjoy it! ❧

FAIRY-TALE GNOME LUNCH

Informal Dinner for Four

INING AT HOME FOR THE FORD FAMILY means an evening spent in style and luxury. Kelli is an interior designer and owner of Madison in Dallas's prestigious Highland Park Village. Although Madison is filled with precious tabletop gems, it is Kelli's flare for putting them together that makes them so special.

For an informal dinner at home, the Fords dined at a table for four underneath their spiral staircase. The table was covered with a custom cloth made from a geometric taupe-and-khaki Ashley Hicks fabric. The interesting fabric was the perfect draping to highlight her collection of beautiful tabletop items. The centerpiece was a dramatic tole palm tree. Arrangements of colorful flowers were placed on the sideboard and around the table to bring life to the setting.

Kelli's tabletop themes are based on an event, a color or a season. In this case, she elaborated on the colors in her incredible Limoges plates with hand-painted figures. They were wonderful conversation pieces because each one was different. Napkins were custom monogrammed by Madison in colors to coordinate with the plates. The oversized lettering gave the table an added bit of drama. Beautiful stemware from the William Yeoward "Isabel" collection graced each setting. Kelli's silver is from Jean E. Puiforcat and the blue glasses are by Artel Glass.

Lighting and scent are additional ways to set the tone of your dinner. Kelli suggests lighting lots of candles and cooking apples with cinnamon in the kitchen for an autumnal dinner, as an example.

Finishing touches are the fun part of decorating a table. In this case, she added a silver shell decoration from Madison to embellish her table. Be playful and creative with the things you place on your table. They could be from any room in the house but when moved to the table, they can make it shine.

ELBOWS ON THE TABLE

Elbows are acceptable on the table as long as there is not any food in front of you! You may rest your elbows on the table in between courses but not in the middle of them.

Sunday Brunch

*I*T IS ALL ABOUT LAYERS AND MIXING IT UP for lifestyle and home stylist Janet Rosell Rice. Although she is always working in various styles and has the opportunity to study them all, her personal style at home is clean and crisp. To avoid a sterile look in the condo she calls home, she relies on layers of texture as well as a mixture of old and new in her interior design and on her tabletops.

Janet has a laid-back entertaining style. She loves Sunday brunch because "everyone is so relaxed on a Sunday morning. People can kick back without a long list of things to do looming over them," she explained.

Janet's dining table—an estate sale find—is magical, with its Lucite legs and black marble top. The chairs, which belonged to her grandmother, have been painted white and their seats re-upholstered in black leather, giving them a modern twist. Janet has a passion for collecting china. For this table, she chose her Hermés "Chaine d'Ancre Blue." She laid the charger, dinner plate and salad plate for presentation and used a rectangular sushi plate in place of the bread plate, which created more room for the delicious breakfast pastries!

Crisp white linen place mats from Sferra Brothers looked beautiful on top of the black tabletop. Janet's monogrammed navy blue napkins with white piping were placed through vintage Hermés napkin rings. To prevent her tabletop from looking too stark, Janet added Rococo to the modern setting in the form of her wedding silver (also her mother's and grandmother's pattern), "Grand Baroque" sterling by Wallace. Her simple and exquisite stemware is the "St. Remy" pattern by Baccarat. Off to the side, a bar cart became a small buffet so guests could easily serve themselves coffee, juice or champagne.

In the center of the table was a stunning arrangement of white flowers by Dallas designer Chris Whanger—enormous white hydrangeas, full white roses and white lilies in rectangular crystal vases. The largest vase was set in the middle and overflowed with opulent flowers, while two smaller ones flanked it. Janet graciously sent each guest home with a miniature version of the center-piece so they could start their week with a smile. ❧

Coral on the Beach

WHEN THE OPPORTUNITY TO DINE ON THE BEACH arises, I am the first to volunteer to participate. I love the sound of the water, the feel of the sand between my toes and watching the dune grass sway in the breeze.

I like to start my dinners on the beach while it is still light outside, leaving the candles unlit. As the sun goes down, I light candles both on the table and around the table for a beautiful glow.

For this party, my husband and our friends carried the teak table and chairs down to the beach for our special sunset dinner. Raynaud's "Cristobal" pattern china seemed a good choice for the evening. I love its color and pattern, and I especially love all of the different pieces that it has; chargers, dinner plates, dessert plates, bread plates, crescent salad plates and serving pieces all came into service that evening. Each piece has a different pattern, some with a coral-colored background and white accents and others with a white background and handpainted coral branches. My favorite pieces in the group are the sea urchin–shaped salt and pepper shakers set on a small square tray.

Simple crystal glassware perfectly complemented our tabletop. A centerpiece of curving driftwood fitted with small containers for tea light candles added to our simple beach look. Large chunks of coral, some set into Lucite bases, added color to the center. Beautiful gold-covered seashells filled in other spaces and highlighted the gold accents on the china. A set of antique glasses with handblown coral accents served as vases. They were filled with sand to help the blowing dune grass stay standing tall.

Finally, smiling guests around the table and the gorgeous light of the sunset were the perfect complements to our coral supper. ❧

Outdoor Entertaining

When serving dinner for special guests outdoors, be sure to think through what their experience might be from start to finish. For example, if it gets chilly on the beach where you spend your holidays, it is a nice gesture to have a pile of pashminas or warm wraps in a basket nearby so your guests can put them around their shoulders as the sun goes down. You might even hang one over the back of each guest's chair and give them as party favors to take home at the end of the evening.

Could guests ruin their shoes in the sand? Ask them to trade in their beautiful shoes for flip-flops that you provide at a "shoe check." Are there nasty biting insects that might visit your table? Place a small but attractive basket of insect repellents in the powder room or on a nearby deck for guests to keep those pesky critters away.

Lobster Lunch on the Lawn

OBSTER LUNCH ON THE LAWN is always a favorite. Who doesn't like to indulge in an afternoon seafood feast? At our lake house, I like to cover the picnic table with a crisp white linen from Porthault. Large white-and-pine chairs are brought from inside to make sure people have plenty of comfortable space to maneuver when dining on these delicacies.

Red beaded place mats from Amen Wardy in Aspen were placed on top of the linen, and large leaf-shaped plates and bowls made the settings. White linen napkins embroidered with a large lobster were folded and placed to the right of each place setting. But with lobster, a napkin is often not enough; lobster bibs were placed in each glass and guests were instructed to tie them on even before the food was brought out.

We placed a red fishing net runner down the center of the table and decorated with silver lobsters and crabs, as well as a pair of white ceramic vases perfect for holding colorful summer dahlias. The dahlias in different shades of reds and orange were selected to complement the colors in the napkins. Coral-handled flatware, also from Amen Wardy, framed the place mats and settings. It was the ideal setting for a delicious lunch, and one that we look forward to every summer. ❧

LOBSTER LUNCH ON THE LAWN

Seashells by the Seashore

RUNCH BY THE SEASHORE is always a delight. A large round table on our deck, often set with comfortable ivory director's chairs, provides a nice place for relaxing. Seashells and shell-inspired items made this a wonderful table setting.

I started with gorgeous woven wicker chargers from Amen Wardy in Aspen. Their elaborate border of seashells was highlighted by the glass seashell plates on top. A matching bread plate to the left of each setting was ready for all of the wonderful pastries that were to be served.

Napkins by Kim Seybert were embroidered with seashells and layered with pale pink organza napkins with a scalloped edge. Mother-of-pearl napkin rings held them together. The simple silverware looked beautiful, but it was the shell spoons that really made the table perfect.

I decorated the center of the table with three dramatic shell-covered obelisks surrounded by various shell-shaped containers filled with shells and flowers. A stunning brass shell was filled with white flowers. A unique Venetian glass shell held seashells collected over the years. Finally, a large collection of luminescent shells scattered across the tabletop glistened in the sun.

The table was relaxing and perfect for our brunch, but the highlight of the meal was set up on a side table where an oversize shell was filled with ice and champagne for a mimosa bar. 🌿

Seashells by the Seashore

Sunflowers for Friends

WHEN THE WEATHER IS NICE and I am planning a lunch for friends, I would much rather meet at a table set outside than at a restaurant. After inviting three friends over for a casual lunch, I picked up a big bunch of sunflowers at the market and set a simple table beside the pool, where we could enjoy the calming sound of the fountains. A large, red, wooden popcorn bowl from Crate & Barrel was the perfect container for these bright yellow stunners.

Woven square place mats framed each setting of simple white plates on a crisp and clean white cloth. While a formal silver set would have been too much for this table setting, the elegant wooden swirl handles of my favorite flatware suited it to perfection. To pull the look together, sunflower print napkins trimmed in red, from Porthault, were carefully placed on each plate. The green glasses with a blue rim were souvenirs from a trip to Mexico.

Our lunch in the garden was perfection and I will continue to make "reservations" at home when I get the chance to enjoy an afternoon with friends. ❧

AL FRESCO

Fourth of July

FAMILY HOLIDAYS LIKE THE FOURTH OF JULY ARE A GREAT EXCUSE to have some fun and set a casual and playful table. All formalities can be thrown aside and you can do what you think your guests will enjoy. At this Fourth of July party, an outdoor table allowed us to enjoy the pretty summer weather and also move easily to a spot on the lawn where we could enjoy the local fireworks display after dark. I love square tables, so I took this chance to rent one for our early dinner. I found wonderful navy fabric with white stars at a wholesale fabric shop and quickly bought up a dozen yards. The talented Nicolas Villalba whipped up a custom cloth, and I was ready to start setting up.

Nothing screams Fourth of July more than watermelon, so to celebrate this refreshing summer fruit I placed three of them in a large galvanized bucket. By cutting the tops off the watermelons, I made a sort of vase out of them and tucked stems of red Gerber daisies right into the moist melons. The flowers stayed fresh much longer than if they had been simply put in water.

A trip to Pottery Barn provided me with the perfect outdoor plates on which to serve our burgers and french fries. These wonderful enameled plates are practically indestructible and I'll use them for many outdoor occasions. I had a hard time deciding how to use charming little white buckets—whether to serve the french fries in them, fill them with ice and a bottled drink or place the flatware and napkins in them. The flatware won the battle, but I know they will find many other uses in the future. We folded red-and-white-striped napkins and placed them inside each bucket as an envelope for the navy-handled flatware. Place cards were made from bright blue paper, white glitter glue and striped ribbon stickers. They were playful and fun, just like our guests!

Above the table, red and white Chinese lanterns hung from the roof of the cabana. These inexpensive but effective lights were the perfect touch for our special outdoor meal.

A basket of insect spray, some little American flags stuck into our potted plants and a lot of lemonade were the finishing touches to our casual get-together. With my husband at the grill and our guests around the pool, we had a fantastic evening.

AL FRESCO

Couples Cabana Lunch

SOMETIMES A SPECIAL OUTDOOR OCCASION requires a little cover, especially in the spring when rain can be just around the corner. A small cabana, like the black-and-white-striped one we used to frame this tabletop, also offers a nice spot of shade from the sun. The cabana inspired me to pull out my black-and-white china as well. Black has recently been such a big trend in china and crystal thanks to Phillipe Starck's famous black crystal chandelier and, later, for the table. The trend has continued, and more and more people are incorporating this great neutral color into their tablescapes. If done right, it can be elegant and whimsical.

For this table, I wanted to introduce another bright color. I chose orange because of the wonderful kumquats that were available, and they became a gorgeous edible centerpiece. The base of the centerpiece, an orangerie box covered in green moss, was filled with a kumquat topiary created by placing the tiny fruits into a cone-shaped form with toothpicks to hold them in place. Green leaves were intermittently placed between the kumquats.

For the rest of the table details, I started with an orange satin tablecloth, which, of course, I did not have in my linen closet. I ordered it from BBJ Linens, a nationwide linen rental company that can accommodate single tables or huge galas. They are a fantastic resource that I keep on speed dial. I had the perfect napkins in my linen closet, though—beautiful white linen monogrammed with a black W. Each guest's place was marked by a white place card with a black border and his or her name expertly written in orange by calligrapher Laurie Harper. Woven flatware was set on the side of charger plates, and the white bowl was perfect for our delicious spring soup, which was also orange.

Tiny ivory porcelain orangerie boxes were placed on the table to add a bit of interest. Gorgeous glassware from Bavaria added an elegant touch as well. The overall effect was charming for a spring couples lunch. ❧

Resources

AUCTIONS

CHRISTIE'S
www.christies.com

DOYLE NEW YORK
www.doylenewyork.com

SOTHEBY'S
www.sothebys.com

TABLETOP

ABC CARPET & HOME
888 & 881 Broadway New York, NY 10003
212.473.3000
www.abchome.com

AMEN WARDY HOME
210 South Galena St.
Aspen, CO 81611
800.228.5987
www.amenwardyaspen.com

BOXWOODS
100 East Andrews Dr.
Atlanta, GA 30305
404.233.3400
www.boxwoodsonline.com

CHARLOTTE MOSS TOWNHOUSE
20 East 63rd St.
New York, NY 10021
212.308.3888
www.charlottemoss.com

D. PORTHAULT
470 Park Ave.
New York, NY 10022
212.688.1660

85A Highland Park Village
Dallas, TX 75205
214.526.3545

CHRISTIAN DIOR PARIS
8, Place Vendome
75001 Paris, France
+33 1 42 96 30 84

E. BRAUN & CO.
717 Madison Ave.
New York, NY 10021
212.838.0650

350 Camden Dr.
Beverly Hills, CA 90210
310.273.4320
www.ebraunandco.com

HERMES
www.Hermes.com

LEONTINE LINENS
Representative: Gigi Lancaster
214.522.3733
gigi@Leontinelinens.com
www.leontinelinens.com

MADISON
45 Highland Park Village, No. A
Dallas, TX 75205
214.528.8118
www.kkmadison.com

MARY MAHONEY
351 Worth Ave.
Palm Beach, FL 33480
561.655.8288
www.marymahoney.com

MAXFIELD
Vintage Hermes
8825 Melrose Ave.
Los Angeles, CA 90069
310.274.8800

MILTON KENT ANTIQUES
2819 N. Henderson Ave.
Dallas, TX 75209
214.826.7553

NATHAN TURNER
636 Almont Dr.
Los Angeles, CA 90069
310.275.1209
www.nathanturner.com

NEIMAN MARCUS
www.neimanmarcus.com

STANLEY KORSHAK HOME STORE
500 Crescent Court
Dallas, TX 75201
800.972.5959
www.stanleykorshak.com

SUE FISHER KING
3067 Sacramento St.
San Francisco, CA
888.881.7276

SUE GRAGG PRECIOUS JEWELS
Silver Chalices
214.630.1422

TIFFANY & CO.
www.Tiffany.com

VIVRE
www.vivre.com

STATIONERS

BERNARD MAISNER
212.477.6776
www.bernardmaisner.com

NEEDLE IN A HAYSTACK
6911 Preston Rd.
Dallas, TX 75205
214.528.2850
www.needleinahaystack.biz

THE PRINTERY
www.iprintery.com
516.922.3250

SMYTHSON
4 West 57th St.
New York, NY 10019
212.265.4573

222 North Rodeo Dr.
Beverly Hills, CA 90210
310.550.1901
www.smythson.com

FLORISTS/EVENT PLANNERS

ANTONY TODD EVENTS
260 West 36th St.
New York, NY 10018
212.367.7363
www.antonytodd.com

ASPEN BRANCH
309A ABC
Aspen, CO 81611
970.925.3791

ATELIER
6819 Snider Plaza
Dallas, TX 75025
214.750.7622

BELLA FLORA
2424 Victory Park Ln.
Dallas, TX 75201
972.445.1200

COLIN COWIE
David Berke
10390 Santa Monica Blvd., Ste. 350
Los Angeles, CA 90025
David@ColinCowie.com

FLEURT FLOWERS
Margaret Ryder
214.350.7676
www.fleurtflowers.com

J & C DESIGN
214.641.7354
www.j-c-design.com

JAYSON HOME AND GARDEN
1885 N Clybourn Ave.
Chicago, IL 60614
800.472.1885

LMD FLORAL BY LEWIS MILLER
437 East 12th St.
New York, NY 10009
212.614.2734
www.LMDFloral.com

MINDY WEISS
232 South Beverly Dr., Ste. 200
Beverly Hills, CA 90212
800.777.3414
310.205.6000
www.mindyweiss.com

PRESTON BAILEY
147 West 25th St., 11th Fl.
New York, NY 10001
212.741.9300
www.prestonbailey.com

SUSAN SPINDLER DESIGNS
214-405-0118

TODD EVENTS
1444 Oak Lawn, Ste. 206
Dallas, TX 75207
214.749.0400
www.toddevents.com

EVENT RENTALS

BBJ LINENS
800.834.0234
www.bbjlinen.com

DUCKY-BOB'S
3200 Belmeade Dr., Suite 130
Carrollton, TX 75006
972.381.8000
800.452.0043
www.duckybobs.com

PARTY RENTAL LTD.
275 North St.
Teterboro, NJ 07608
888.PR.HIPPO
201.727.4700
www.partyrentalltd.com

RSVP SOIREE EVENT RENTALS
1937 Irving Blvd.
Dallas, TX 75207
214.350.7787
www.DallasRSVP.com

SUITE 206
1444 Oak Lawn, Ste. 206
Dallas, TX 75207
214.749.0400 x104
www.suite206.com

UNIQUE TABLETOP RENTALS
800.709.7007
www.uniquetabletoprentals.com

Photographer Credits